Monster Megan's BIG Clean Up

By Dee Reid

Reading Consultant: Beth Walker Gambro

Ruby Tuesday Books

Published in 2018 by Ruby Tuesday Books Ltd.

Copyright © 2018 Ruby Tuesday Books Ltd.

Design and illustrations: Emma Randall
Editor: Ruth Owen
Production: John Lingham

Library of Congress Control Number: 2018946145
Print (hardback) ISBN 978-1-78856-050-4
Print (paperback) ISBN 978-1-78856-069-6
eBook ISBN 978-1-78856-051-1

Printed and published in the United States of America.

For further information including rights and permissions requests, please contact our Customer Services Department at 877-337-8577.

4

It is a mess.

5

Mo must clean up things in the shape of a circle.

Max must clean up things in the shape of a triangle.

OK.

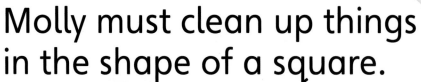

Molly must clean up things in the shape of a square.

OK.

15

But who will clean up things in the shape of a rectangle?

It is great fun to clean up.

18

Now, it is all very neat.

squares

triangles

Great job, monsters.

rectangles

circles

21

Can you see three things
in the shape of a triangle?

How many things are in
the shape of a rectangle?

22

What shapes can you see in the house?

Can you remember?

Why did Megan tell the monsters to clean up?

How did Megan make cleaning up fun?

Who cleaned up things in the shape of a rectangle?

Do you like cleaning up?

Can you read these words?

in it must of up we